World War II: 133 Fascinating Facts For Kids

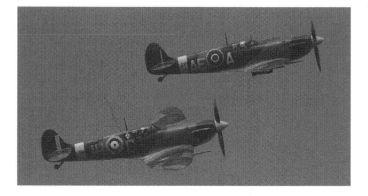

David Railton

This book is just one of a series of "Fascinating Facts For Kids" books. For more fascinating facts about people, history, animals and more please visit:

www.fascinatingfactsforkids.com

Contents

Why the War Started

1. Following the defeat of Germany in World War I, the victorious nations drew up the Treaty of Versailles, which was meant to stop any future wars taking place.

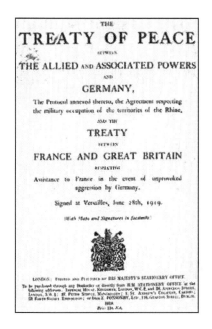

2. The treaty blamed Germany for starting the war and made her pay huge fines. It also stated that Germany was not allowed to rebuild her Army and Navy.

3. The German people thought that the treaty was too harsh and they felt humiliated, but their leaders agreed to sign it in order to end the war.

4. World War I was now over but the British Prime Minister, David Lloyd George, was uneasy about Germany's humiliation and remarked, "We shall have to do the whole thing again in 20 years time." He was to be proved right.

5. The German economy was in ruins with millions of people having no jobs or money, but a former soldier called Adolf Hitler offered them a solution to their problems.

6. Hitler was the leader of a political party called the National Socialists, or "Nazis", and he promised to make Germany great again if the people voted for him.

Adolf Hitler

7. Hitler came to power in 1933 and set about rebuilding the Army to go to war again. He planned to build a German empire, called the "Third Reich", which he said would last for 1,000 years.

8. Germany wasn't the only country in Europe to see the rise of a dictator like Hitler. Benito Mussolini in Italy and Joseph Stalin in Russia took advantage of their own countries' problems to take power. And in the Far East, Japan, like Germany, was looking to create her own empire using military force.

Hitler's Germany

9.   Hitler believed that people with German blood were superior to other races. He was determined to conquer the non-German countries of Europe and also destroy the Jewish people, who he thought were responsible for all Germany's problems.

10.   There were over half a million Jews living in Germany at the time and when the Nazis came to power those working in the government and at universities were thrown out of their jobs. Many Jews were put in prison and were often bullied in the streets.

11.   On the night of November 9 1938 Jewish homes and shops were attacked all over Germany in what became known as "Kristallnacht", or "Night of the Broken Glass".

The day after "Kristallnacht"

12. The Nazis convinced the German people of their policies by organizing massive rallies where Hitler's speeches captivated the crowd. The newspapers, radio and cinemas were all full of Nazi propaganda to brainwash the population.

13. The minds of children were also corrupted as Nazi policies were taught in schools. Boys were expected to join an organization called the "Hitler Youth", where they learned how to be soldiers. Girls joined the "League of Maidens", where they were taught to be good Nazi wives and mothers, producing boys for Hitler's Army.

Hitler Youth at rifle practice

14. The Nazis created many jobs for the German people as new roads and government buildings were built. New factories produced weapons and military equipment, and the size of the Army was greatly increased. Germany was becoming a rich and powerful country once more.

The Road to War

15. In 1931 Japan began her empire building by invading the Chinese region of Manchuria. Other countries protested but Japan ignored them and declared war on China.

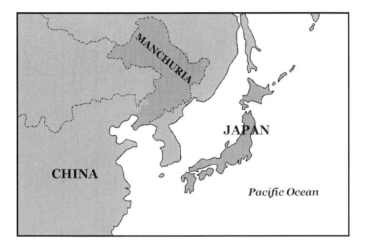

16. In 1935 Italy invaded the East African country of Abyssinia, now called Ethiopia. The Italian Army used aircraft and poison gas against barefooted African tribesmen, but it still took 8 months to defeat the Abyssinians.

17. In 1936 Hitler's Army took control of the Rhineland, the area separating France and Germany. 2 years later Austria was invaded and united with Germany. Both these actions had been forbidden by the Treaty of Versailles, but Hitler was taking revenge for the humiliation of Germany 20 years earlier.

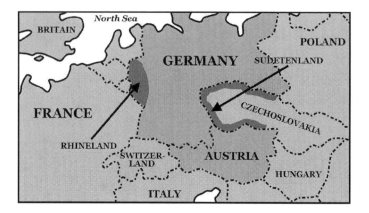

18. In August 1938 Hitler demanded that a German-speaking part of Czechoslovakia, the Sudetenland, should become part of Germany. In talks with the British and French Prime Ministers, this demand was granted when Hitler promised that he would take no more territory. Hitler was not telling the truth as his Army marched into the Czech capital, Prague, in March 1939.

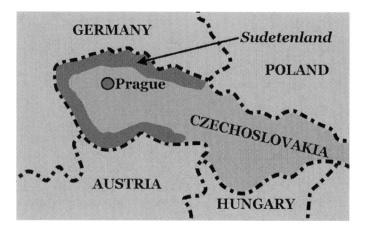

19. Hitler now turned his attention further east to Poland, believing that the British and French would do nothing to stop him.

20. Nazi soldiers flooded into Poland on September 1 1939. Hitler was wrong about Britain and France, as these 2 countries declared war on Germany. Europe was now at war again, just 20 years after the end of the bloodiest conflict in history. The war that was to come would be even worse, lasting 6 long years and claiming 50 million lives.

21. Countries from all across the world would eventually become involved in the war. On one side were the Axis powers, led by Germany, Italy and Japan and on the other side were the Allies, which included Great Britain, the United States, France and Russia.

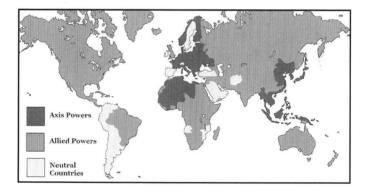

The divided world in 1942

The Fall of France

22. Britain sent an army and fighter aircraft to mainland Europe to help defend France against the expected German invasion. Germany had invaded Norway and Denmark in April 1940 before turning her attention to France.

23. Following World War I, the French had spent an enormous amount of money building a long line of heavy fortifications on their border with Germany to repel any invasion. It was called the Maginot Line and was to prove a total failure.

24. On May 10 Hitler invaded Holland, Belgium and Luxembourg, approaching France from the north and ignoring the Maginot Line completely.

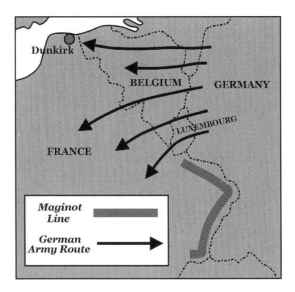

25. The British and French Armies were beaten back and the British retreated to the port of Dunkirk on the French coast. Hitler had them at his mercy, but for some reason he ordered his Army to halt.

26. Hitler's strange decision gave the British time to get her soldiers back to England. Hundreds of boats of all sizes sailed across the English Channel to Dunkirk and were able to rescue over 300,000 British soldiers.

27. Dunkirk has gone down in British history as a glorious and heroic episode, but to the French it was a betrayal, as Hitler's Army was now free to march on the French capital, Paris.

28. The Germans entered Paris on June 14 and France surrendered a week later. During World War I, Germany had spent 4 years trying to defeat France, but Hitler had managed it in less than 6 weeks.

Hitler (center) in Paris

The Battle of Britain

29. Hitler's next target was Britain, but the English Channel, which separated England from the rest of Europe, posed a problem. Ships carrying the German Army across the Channel would be easy targets for British fighter aircraft, so Hitler decided that the British Royal Air Force (the RAF) had to be destroyed.

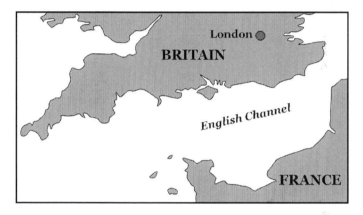

30. The German Air Force, the "Luftwaffe", began to attack ships in the English Channel. The plan was to draw British aircraft into the skies above the Channel where they could be shot down. The head of the Luftwaffe, Hermann Goering, boasted that this tactic would destroy the RAF in 4 days.

31. Goering's plan didn't succeed as the RAF was able to shoot down twice as many aircraft as the Luftwaffe could manage.

32. Goering changed tactics and ordered his pilots to attack British airfields and destroy aircraft while they were still on the ground. This plan did work, as the RAF suffered heavy losses of both aircraft and men.

33. The British responded by sending bombers to drop bombs on the German capital, Berlin. Hitler was furious and ordered Goering to retaliate by bombing London. But this change of tactics gave the RAF time to repair its airfields and replace its lost aircraft.

34. The Germans bombed London and other British cities night after night for months during what became known as the "Blitz", which is the German word for "lightning".

Firefighters after a German bombing

35. Every day in the skies over southern England, the RAF fighter aircraft, including Spitfires and Hurricanes, fought a fierce battle against the German bombers and fighters.

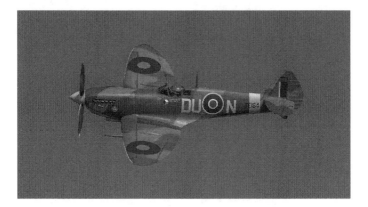

A British Spitfire

36. In the end, the RAF shot down 1700 enemy aircraft and lost 900. The Germans finally admitted defeat and Hitler abandoned his plans to invade Britain.

37. The RAF lost 400 of its 1500 pilots during the "Battle of Britain", including men from other allied countries such as Poland and Czechoslovakia. The British Prime Minister, Winston Churchill, saluted the pilots with the words, "Never in the field of human conflict was so much owed by so many to so few."

Winston Churchill

Operation Barbarossa

38. Despite the setback against Britain, Hitler felt invincible and on June 22 1941 he ordered the start of the greatest invasion the world had ever seen.

39. "Operation Barbarossa" was the codename for the invasion of the world's largest country, Russia, by more than 3 million German soldiers and thousands of aircraft and tanks. Hitler was so confident that he expected Russia to fall by the end of the summer.

40. The Germans invaded Russia in 3 groups - north towards Leningrad, south towards Ukraine and through the middle towards the Russian capital, Moscow.

German routes
into Russia ⟶

41. The German Armies advanced rapidly, but
the Russians fought fiercely and it wasn't until
October that the outskirts of Leningrad and
Moscow were reached.

42. Winter soon came and brought heavy snow and temperatures as low as -30°C (-22°F). The extreme cold stopped weapons, tanks and trucks from working, and wearing just their summer uniforms, countless German soldiers froze to death.

43. The Russians had fought bravely to protect their homeland and the exhausted Germans couldn't carry on. Operation Barbarossa had been a failure, with Hitler's Army suffering a terrible defeat and Moscow being saved from the Nazis.

Pearl Harbor

44. Pearl Harbor was a massive naval base on one of the Hawaiian Islands in the middle of the Pacific Ocean. It was the headquarters of the United States' Pacific Fleet.

45. Japan wanted to take control of the Pacific region but the powerful United States Navy stood in her way, so a plan was devised to destroy the American fleet.

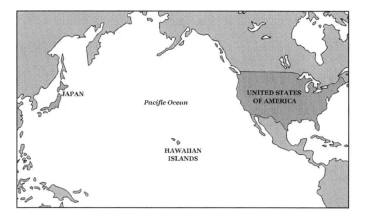

The Pacific region

46. In November 1941 Japanese aircraft carriers set sail secretly for a point in the Pacific Ocean 300 miles (480 km) north of the Hawaiian Islands. From this distance Japanese aircraft could launch an attack on Pearl Harbor.

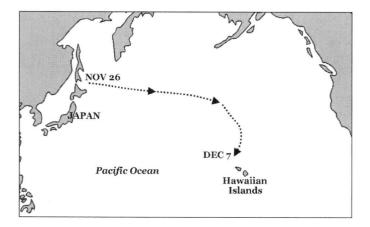

47. Early on the quiet Sunday morning of December 7, the peace was broken as wave after wave of Japanese aircraft attacked the naval base.

48. The Americans were caught completely by surprise and could offer little defense as the Japanese aircraft caused terrible destruction.

49. 30 minutes after they had appeared, the Japanese aircraft vanished from the sky before heading back for a second attack half an hour later. This second strike was less successful, as the Americans were now ready and able to use their anti-aircraft guns.

50. By the end of the attack the Japanese had managed to destroy 18 American warships and nearly 200 aircraft with the loss of 2,400 lives and 1,000 wounded.

51. Nearly half the casualties of the attacks were aboard the battleship "Arizona", which was hit 4 times before eventually sinking. During the first attack a bomb fell straight down the Arizona's funnel, setting off a massive explosion which killed 1,000 men.

The "Arizona" after the Japanese attack

52. Despite the massive damage inflicted by the Japanese, the operation was not a complete success. The most important warships of the United States Navy, the aircraft carriers, were not at Pearl Harbor at the time of the attack. They were safely at sea and so the American Navy was still in business.

53. The United States was outraged by the attack on Pearl Harbor and declared war on Japan. As a fellow Axis power, Germany then declared war on the United States. This was great news for Britain and her allies, as they now had the most powerful nation on Earth fighting beside them.

54. Following Pearl Harbor, Japan knew that she had to build her new empire before the American Navy could get back to full strength again. She wasted no time, invading many Pacific territories, including countries which were part of the British Empire.

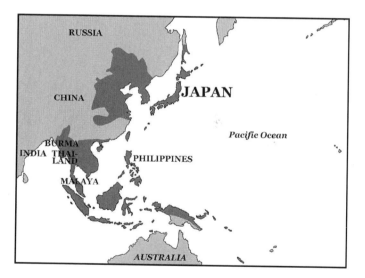

The Japanese Empire in 1942

55. Malaya, the Philippines, Thailand and Burma all fell to the well-trained Japanese Army and even India and Australia feared a Japanese invasion.

56. Japan seemed as powerful and unstoppable in the Pacific as Hitler was in Europe, but in the spring of 1942 America was preparing to strike back in revenge for the devastating attack on Pearl Harbor.

The Battle of the Atlantic

57. The richest country in the world, the United States of America, was able to produce more ships, aircraft and weapons than any other nation. But all this military equipment had to get to Britain across the Atlantic Ocean so that it could be used against Hitler.

58. Allied cargo ships full of military hardware and other supplies sailed from America in large groups, or "convoys", protected by Navy warships. Their 3,000 mile (4,800 km) voyage was a dangerous one, as waiting for them were German submarines, the "U-boats".

A German U-boat

59. Britain's very survival depended on the convoys getting through, so the Germans were determined to sink as many allied ships as they could before they reached their destinations.

60. At the beginning of the war, the U-boats were very successful as they roamed the Atlantic Ocean in packs, using their torpedoes to attack the allied convoys. At one stage they were sinking nearly 100 ships every month, a number that the Allies could not afford to lose. They attacked at night when they couldn't be seen and on the surface where underwater detecting equipment couldn't find them.

61. It looked as if the Germans were going to win not just the Battle of the Atlantic, but the war itself. But in 1942 British scientists broke a secret German code which gave away the positions of the U-boats. Also, radar was used to detect U-boats on the surface. This radar was so successful that the U-boats were forced to attack from underwater where it was more difficult to fire their torpedoes accurately.

62. These breakthroughs gave the Allies a huge advantage and by May 1943 the Battle of the Atlantic was won.

63. Nearly 1,200 U-boats fought in the Atlantic Ocean but the Allies managed to sink 800 of them. The Allies had lost many ships and lives early on in the war, but by 1944 2 million tons of military equipment had crossed the Atlantic, as well as nearly 2 million American soldiers, to help the British in the fight against Hitler.

America Strikes Back

64. By the spring of 1942 Japan was at the height of her powers and planning the invasion of Australia and the American islands of Hawaii. The United States Navy though, had recovered from the attack on Pearl Harbor and America was looking for revenge.

65. In May 1942 the Japanese fleet set sail for the southern tip of New Guinea, from where it would launch the invasion of Australia.

66. The United States Navy knew what Japan was up to and prepared to ambush them. They intercepted the Japanese in the Coral Sea and launched an attack.

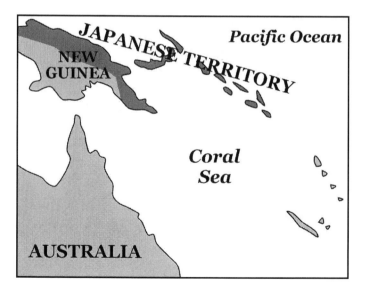

67. At the Battle of Coral Sea, which lasted from May 4-8, neither the Japanese nor the American fleets actually saw each other. All the fighting was carried out by aircraft flying from aircraft carriers.

68. Although the Japanese sunk one American aircraft carrier and shot down 65 airplanes, their own losses were nearly double that. The Japanese Navy had been dealt a serious blow.

69. Japan pressed on with her invasion plans by sending a fleet to the Central Pacific island of Midway, where the United States had a naval base. From there it was just 600 miles (965 km) to Hawaii.

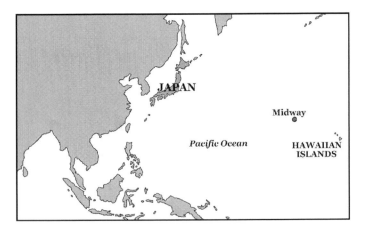

70. The United States Navy was once again laying in wait and on June 4 the Americans launched a massive attack on the Japanese from aircraft carriers and the airfields on Midway.

71. In the space of just 6 minutes, 3 Japanese aircraft carriers were sunk and another badly damaged. The Americans lost just one ship, the "Yorktown".

72. The Battle of Midway was the turning point of the war in the Pacific, as the Japanese Navy was dealt a fatal blow. The United States Navy was now in control of the Pacific Ocean.

73. Over the next 3 years the United States Navy and her allies were to win back much of the territory seized by Japan. The Japanese fought fiercely and savagely but the Allies took island after island as they battled their way to mainland Japan.

The Desert War & the Italian Campaign

74. Italy had entered the war in June 1940 and in September of that year she attacked British forces in Egypt. Britain retaliated by attacking the Italian colonies of Libya and Italian East Africa.

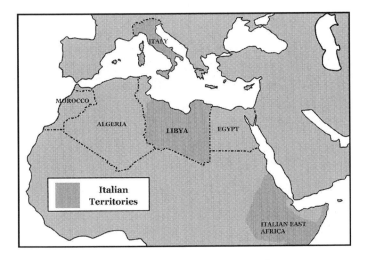

75. The British were threatening to capture the whole of North Africa, so Hitler was forced to send help to his Italian allies.

76. In the spring of 1941 the German Afrika Korps landed in Libya under the command of Field Marshal Erwin Rommel. His Army advanced east and pushed the British back towards Egypt. Now it was the Germans that were threatening to take over the whole of North Africa.

77. Over the next 2 years the 2 Armies pushed each other back and forth across the African desert. By August 1942 the British troops were exhausted, but were given a new lease of life with the appointment of an inspiring new commander, General Bernard Montgomery, known simply as "Monty".

General Montgomery

78. During the summer both Armies took up positions at the Egyptian town of El Alamein. In October the German Army lost Rommel, who was sent back to Germany ill with exhaustion. The Army also lost the protection of the Air

Force, as most of the aircraft had been sent to help out in Russia.

79. On October 23 Montgomery took advantage by launching a massive attack. 1,000 guns bombarded the Afrika Korps before British soldiers and tanks forced the Germans to retreat. The next month, more allied troops landed in Morocco and Algeria. The Germans were caught in the middle of 2 allied Armies and in May 1943 they surrendered.

80. With no more German opposition the allied forces were able to sail across the Mediterranean Sea to the Italian island of Sicily, which was captured within 5 weeks.

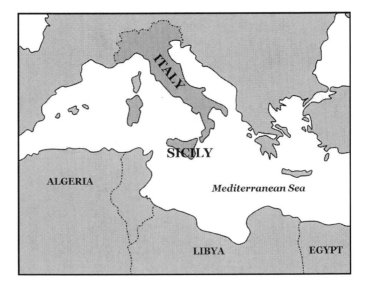

81. The Italian government surrendered to the Allies in September 1943 and the invasion of the Italian mainland, which was full of German soldiers, could begin.

82. 6 days after the surrender, American troops landed at Salerno on the south-western coast of the Italian mainland. It took 9 months of heavy fighting before the Allies reached the Italian capital, Rome, but they didn't get much further as the German Army held on to northern Italy until the end of the war.

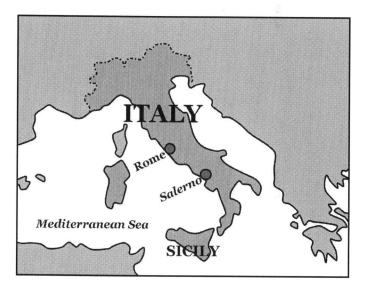

The Battle of Stalingrad

83. Following the unsuccessful campaigns at Leningrad and Moscow, Hitler ordered his Army south to capture the oil fields of the Caucasus region. Between the Germans and the oil fields stood the city of Stalingrad.

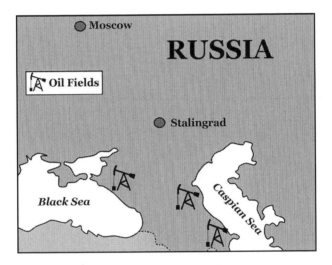

84. The German Army reached the outskirts of Stalingrad in August 1942, led by General Friedrich von Paulus. Paulus had 200,000 men under his command and was confident of a quick victory against the 50,000 strong Russian Army.

85. On August 23 the Army and 600 German bombers attacked the city, killing 40,000 people on that day alone. The bombs, though, were turning the city into rubble which would provide ideal conditions for the Russians to fight in.

86. The Russians defended their city with great bravery and heroism, and by early October were showing no signs of surrender. Paulus ordered what he hoped would be one final attack, but the appearance of Russian reinforcements meant that the attack failed.

87. Winter was now approaching and as at Moscow the previous year, the Germans were unprepared for the extreme cold. Once again, German soldiers were freezing to death in their summer uniforms.

88. The Russians now prepared to counter-attack and within a week the German Army was surrounded. On February 2 they surrendered and the Russians took 90,000 men prisoner. In Stalingrad, only one in a hundred buildings was left standing.

The center of Stalingrad after the battle

The Holocaust

89. Hitler and the Nazis hated the Jewish people, who they blamed for all of Germany's problems. Hitler was determined to rid Germany of the Jews.

90. When Hitler came to power in 1933, he had encouraged the German people to use violence against the Jews and to destroy their property.

91. When the war broke out in 1939, Jews were expelled from Germany to countries that the Germans had conquered. They were forced to live in appalling conditions in special areas of cities known as "ghettos".

92. Many Jews were murdered by the Nazis with hundreds being shot at a time. In 1941, at Babi Yar in Russia, 33,000 Jews were shot and killed in the space of 3 days. By the end of the year, over one million Jews had been murdered.

93. These mass killings took time and were difficult to keep secret from both local people and the rest of the world. A different way of getting rid of the Jews was needed.

94. In 1942 Nazi leaders came up with a new plan. It was decided that all Jews in Nazi occupied Europe would be sent to special "death camps" where they would be gassed to death.

95. The Nazis built several death camps in Poland and Jews from all over Nazi Europe were rounded up and told that they were going to be "resettled".

96. Jews arrived at the death camps by train. The healthier men and women were chosen to work in factories and used as slave labor, but the rest were herded into rooms which were then locked, before poison gas was poured through the ceilings.

Prisoners in the death camp at Auschwitz

97. When everyone was dead, gold teeth and rings were removed and melted down before the bodies were burned.

98. During the 6 years of World War II, as many as 6 million Jews were murdered at the death camps in what became known as the "Holocaust", surely the worst crime in all human history.

The Bombing of Germany

99. In February 1942 the RAF began bombing German cities in night-time raids. The aim of targeting ordinary civilians instead of military targets was to break the morale of the German people.

100. The US Army Air Force, which was using air bases in Britain, was flying during the day and dropping bombs on military and industrial targets.

A British "Lancaster" bomber

101. Both the British and American Air Forces suffered heavy losses. Their slow and heavy bombers were vulnerable to attack by German fighter aircraft and exposed to the accurate anti-aircraft weapons on the ground. On one raid on a ball-bearing factory, more than 60 American bombers were shot down.

102. The allied losses began to decline from 1944, when new long-range fighter aircraft were able to escort the bombers to Germany and back, as well as keeping the German Air Force at bay.

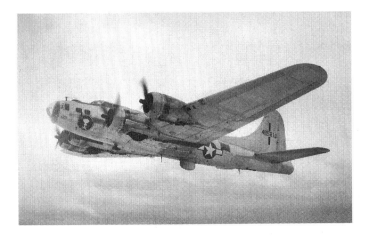

An American "B-17 Flying Fortress"

103. By the end of the war, nearly every industrial town and city in Germany had suffered massive bomb damage, with Hamburg and Dresden being virtually destroyed. It was on February 13 1945, that nearly 30,000 people died on the raid on Dresden. The British insisted that the city was a legitimate target, but many saw it as a war crime.

Dresden after the bombing

104. At least 300,000 German civilians were killed by the allied bombings, but it seemed to have if little effect on their morale. Like the British during the Blitz back in 1940, the destruction and hardship they suffered made them more determined than ever to carry on.

Operation Overlord

105.   Hitler was struggling in the east against
the Russians, in Italy to the south against British,
Americans and Canadians, and now the Allies
were planning an invasion in the west along the
French coast. The German armed forces were
being stretched to breaking point.

106.   The planned invasion of France was
named "Operation Overlord" and its aim was to
reach the German capital, Berlin, and to free
Europe from the Nazi occupation by defeating
Hitler's Army.

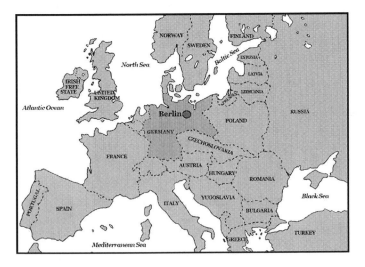

107.   The American general, Dwight D.
Eisenhower, was put in charge of Operation
Overlord. One of the most important decisions

he had to make was choosing the landing point for the invasion of France.

General Dwight D. Eisenhower

108. The French port of Calais was the obvious place for the allied Armies to land as it was not far from the English coast, just over 20 miles (30 km) away.

109. Calais was very heavily defended by the Germans, so Eisenhower decided to land his Armies on the beaches of Normandy, 150 miles (240 km) to the south. Although this would involve a longer sea crossing, the large flat Normandy beaches were perfect for getting large numbers of men and machines ashore quickly.

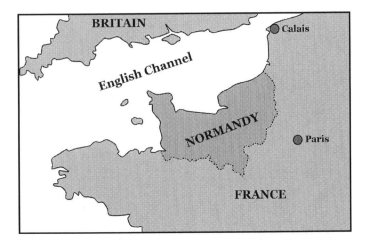

110. A huge force of men, vehicles and weapons were assembled in southern England in preparation for the invasion of France, which was set for June 5 1944 - known as "D-Day".

111. Before the invasion began, General Eisenhower began a campaign of deception against the Germans. Fake Army bases were built in Kent, just across the English Channel from Calais, to make the Germans think that the invasion would start at Calais. Fake coded messages were also sent out to add to the deception.

112. Bad weather meant that the invasion started a day late on June 6, as the largest invasion force in history began its journey across the English Channel from England to France.

113. The Americans came ashore on beaches code-named "Utah" and "Omaha", and the

British and Canadians on beaches called "Gold", "Juno" and "Sword".

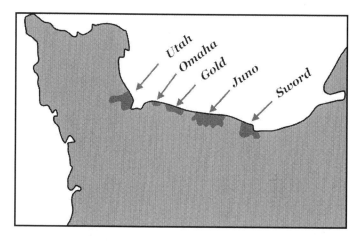

114. There was strong German resistance with 1,000 Americans being killed at Omaha beach, but by the end of the day 150,000 allied soldiers had landed in Normandy with loss of 2,500 lives.

115. Allied troops kept pouring across the English Channel and by the end of June, Eisenhower had 850,000 men in France. It was surely now a question of not if Germany could be beaten, but how long it would take.

From Normandy to Berlin

116. It took the allied Armies 6 weeks to break away from their Normandy landing zones, but when they did, the German resistance crumbled and the way to the French capital, Paris, was clear.

117. The Allies entered Paris to cheering crowds on August 25 and the Germans surrendered at 2.30 that afternoon.

The liberation of Paris

118. With Paris liberated, the Allies continued their march to Berlin, liberating the Belgian cities of Antwerp and Brussels on the way. The German border was crossed on September 11 where a pause took place as fresh supplies were brought in.

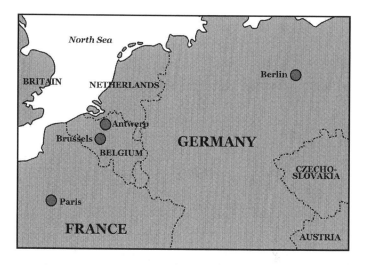

119. When the Allies continued their advance the Germans launched a surprise attack in thick woodland. Tanks swept through snow and fog, causing the Allies to retreat in confusion.

120. Hitler was taking a big gamble as it was his last chance to win the war. Fortunately for the Allies, the weather improved and the clear blue skies allowed the allied Air Forces to batter the German Army into submission. The way to Berlin was now clear.

The Fall of Berlin

121. While the Allies were advancing on Berlin from the west, the Russians were approaching from the east, driving the enemy out of their country and killing 300,000 German soldiers as they did so.

122. By February 1945 the Russians had reached the River Oder, just one hour away from Berlin, where they built up their strength for an assault on the city.

123. The Allies who had landed in Normandy were also close to Berlin, but Eisenhower had decided to allow the Russians to have the glory of taking the city because of his fears of huge casualties.

124.   The Battle for Berlin began on April 16 and a week later the Russians had surrounded the city.

125.   Hitler's generals knew the war was lost and they urged their leader to surrender, but he refused. Instead, he took refuge in an underground bunker beneath government buildings with his guards and his new wife, Eva Braun.

126.   With the Russians ruthlessly taking control of Berlin high above his head, Hitler finally admitted defeat and he and Eva Braun took their own lives. Hitler shot himself in the head and his wife poisoned herself.

127.   The Battle for Berlin saw the deaths of 450,000 German soldiers, 80,000 Russians and 125,000 civilians. The Germans finally surrendered on May 7 1945 and the war in Europe was over after 6 long years.

The Defeat of Japan

128.   With the war now over in Europe, the Allies could turn their full attention to Japan. By June 1945, the Americans were just 350 miles (560 km) from the Japanese mainland and ready to invade.

129.   The Americans had their doubts about invading Japan, fearing the loss of half a million lives, but the United States had a plan to end the war in an instant.

130.   For years, American scientists had been developing the most powerful bomb the world had ever seen - the atomic bomb. Following a successful test in the early summer of 1945, where the explosion had sent a plume of smoke 40,000 feet into the sky, the bomb could now be used on Japan.

131.   The Americans chose the city of Hiroshima as the target for the atomic bomb. It was home to weapons factories, shipyards and a population of 300,000.

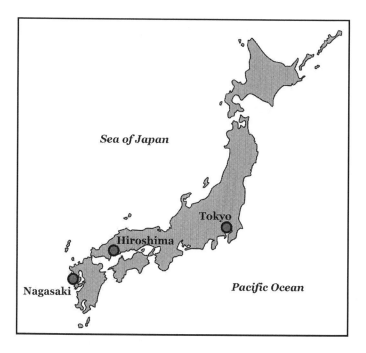

132. At 8.00am on August 6 1945 an American bomber flew over Hiroshima and dropped the bomb. 80,000 people were killed instantly and the city was flattened. 80,000 more were to die over the coming weeks from their injuries and radiation poisoning.

The atomic bomb explodes over Hiroshima

133. Three days after Hiroshima the Japanese still hadn't surrendered and a second bomb was dropped, this time on the city of Nagasaki, with similar results. Five days later, on August 15 1945, the Japanese finally agreed to surrender. World War II was over at last.

Conclusion

World War II was the most destructive conflict in history, claiming at least 50 million lives and making millions more homeless.

After 2 years of relentless bombing by the Allies and invasions from the west and east, Germany was a devastated country.

To avoid another war in the future, the United States provided huge amounts of money and aid to rebuild the shattered countries of Europe.

Russia came out of the war in control of the whole of Eastern Europe and became a bitter rival of the United States. This rivalry threatened yet another war, with weapons even more powerful than the bombs which fell on Hiroshima and Nagasaki.

The legacy of World War II lasted for the rest of the 20th century and is still with us today.

Illustration Attributions

The Treaty of Versailles (Fact 1)
Kallen2021 [CC BY-SA 4.0
(https://creativecommons.org/licenses/by-sa/4.0)]

Adolf Hitler
Bundesarchiv, Bild 183-S33882 / CC BY-SA 3.0 DE
[CC BY-SA 3.0 de
(https://creativecommons.org/licenses/by-sa/3.0/de/deed.en)]

The day after "Kristallnacht"
Bundesarchiv, Bild 146-1970-083-42 / CC-BY-SA 3.0
[CC BY-SA 3.0 de
(https://creativecommons.org/licenses/by-sa/3.0/de/deed.en)]

Hitler Youth at rifle practice
Bundesarchiv, Bild 146-1978-013-27 / Hamann / CC-BY-SA 3.0 [CC BY-SA 3.0 de
(https://creativecommons.org/licenses/by-sa/3.0/de/deed.en)]

Hitler in Paris
National Archives at College Park [Public domain]

Firefighters after a German bombing
New York Times Paris Bureau Collection [Public domain]

Winston Churchill
British Government [Public domain]

A German U-boat
Augusto Ferrer-Dalmau [CC BY-SA 3.0
(https://creativecommons.org/licenses/by-sa/3.0)]

The center of Stalingrad after the battle
RIA Novosti archive, image #602161 / Zelma / CC-
BY-SA 3.0 [CC BY-SA 3.0
(https://creativecommons.org/licenses/by-sa/3.0)]

Prisoners in the death camp at Auschwitz
Unknown, assumed to be the work of the Red Army
[Public domain]

A British "Lancaster" bomber
Photo: Cpl Phil Major ABIPP/MOD [OGL v1.0
(http://NationalArchives.gov.uk/doc/open-
government-licence/version/1/)]

An American "B-17 Flying Fortress"
US Air Force

Dresden after the bombing
Deutsche Fotothek? [CC BY-SA 3.0 de
(https://creativecommons.org/licenses/by-
sa/3.0/de/deed.en)]

General Dwight D. Eisenhower
Official photographer [Public domain]

The liberation of Paris
Jack Downey, U.S. Office of War Information [Public
domain]

The atomic bomb explodes over Hiroshima
509th Operations Group [Public domain]

Made in the USA
Coppell, TX
27 March 2020

17849164R00033